Et in Arcadia Ego.

INTERNAL
CORRESPONDENCE

of

THE PRIORY OF SION

Psalm 87:2

"The LORD loves the gates of Zion..."

Contents

Acknowledgements 7

Foreword 8-9

E.M. 1st Declaration 10-17

E.M. 2nd Declaration 18-29

E.M. – Priory 30-36

E.M. – Paul Wylie 37-39

P.W. Announcement 40-43

P.W. – Priory 44-45

Priory Documents 46-81

Supplementary Material 82-95

Afterword 96

Acknowledgements

These messages are reproduced with the kind permission of Eric Mader-Lin, G.M. P.o.S. You may find more of his work at:
http://www.necessaryprose.com

His published work includes:

- A Taipei Mutt, SARU Press (January 1, 2005)
- Gospels From the Last Man: The Complete Deeds and Sayings of Cosmo Di Madison (Self-published, 1996)
- Idiocy, Ltd. (CreateSpace Independent Publishing Platform; 1 edition (June 14, 2015)

Foreword

This has been a tedious labour of love. I should sue the Priory of Sion for the damage that being bent over these 97 pages has done to my poor neck!

I began this project back in September, 2013 and have officially finished the deciphering on: 28/05/14, 17:37pm. There are no great secrets contained herein. Why would there be?

In the beginning, I was going against the wishes of the Priory in deciphering and publishing. I have since got permission from the Grand Master himself to publish nearly all the deciphered Priory Correspondence, and have even been accepted into the Priory. (On more meaningful terms than Mr. de Ouchy in Letter 13 below.) For reasons I cannot divulge here I was not granted permission to publish the last of the letters, Letter 17. I include the text of that letter here only in its ciphered form.

The whole collection of letters in their ciphered form were posted online in 2006 and can be accessed at:

http://www.necessaryprose.com/prior
ydocuments.htm

If I have learned anything from this
experience, it's that holding back
achieves nothing. Enjoy this book, and
don't take it too seriously.

Also, included in this third edition are
interviews with members of the Priory
of Sion.

Your friend,

Seneschal Wylie, P.o.S.

Eric Mader's First Declaration

Why do you come here, reader? Do you expect to find another review of *The Da Vinci Code*? The hassle and hubbub that book has brought us, you can't imagine. Perhaps you expect to read here once again that Brown's book is an accomplished thriller, but that the author got half his historical facts wrong and sketched out a huge and absurd conspiracy where none was to be found. Is this what you're looking for? How many articles and books have gone over this same ground? Or is it maybe a movie review you expect?

In any case reviews are not what I'm going to offer. What I will write here is far more momentous. I'm going to uncover a secret in the real world--a secret I've kept for years but have finally tired of keeping. With this brief declaration I intend to tell the truth as it is. And so. . . .

I am the Grand Master of the Priory of Sion.

There--I've said it. You may have a hard time believing it, but your scepticism won't change the fact. I am the current Grand Master and have been so for nearly a decade. Frankly I'm getting sick of all the secrecy.

The truth is I've been burning to tell about the Priory ever since they inducted me as an undergrad during my junior year abroad in France. But they insisted I keep my mouth shut, both there at the meeting house off the Rue de la Violette in Aix, and then back in the States as I finished my degree and moved up the ranks. I was persuaded to keep quiet and I was even threatened.

"It's a *secret society*," they'd tell me, pulling grave looks. "We protect an *ancient secret*. Any breach of the secret by a member will be *severely punished*."

Yeah, right. Even then I suspected the worst punishment those French frat boys could dole out would be forcing me to reread their "mystical" poems. Now that I'm Grand Master, I'm not afraid of the Priory rank and file and their silly threats. Besides, of the three *sénéchaux* I know for a fact that two are as tired of all this as I am. I'm unable to keep up the game any longer. With the recent craze and speculation surrounding Brown's book, with all the misconceptions floating around, the need to reveal the truth has only gotten more acute. And so I will come out with it.

The Grand Master is me. I'm the man you're looking for. You wouldn't know it on the surface--actually I hold down a pretty normal job--but then that's just how it should be with a Grand Master. It's the 3 D's: *discretion, deniability, . . .*   I've forgotten the third one.

But enough about me. I should get to some of the good stuff, those questions that keep you up nights, that animate your dinner parties and echo round your chat rooms. *Was Mary Magdalene really the wife of Jesus Christ? Did the Knights Templar really uncover the Temple Treasure in Jerusalem at the time of the First Crusade? Do we Priory members*

12

*really worship the sacred feminine and
engage in ritual sex? Do we really know
where the Holy Grail is hidden? Is there
really a sacred bloodline running from Jesus
through the Merovingian kings and Pierre
Plantard?*

As for Mary Magdalene and Jesus, the
truth is that not even I, the Grand
Master, can tell you reliably about that
one. And the reason is simple. The
Priory of Sion doesn't go back that far,
nor did our Founders (rest their
maligned souls) ever come upon any
secret gospels or any Temple Treasure
either. Sorry to disappoint you. But
what did you expect?

As for the ritual sex, you'll be glad to
know that that part of Brown's book is
mostly true. Except that during the
Hieros Gamos the dancers do not hold
"golden orbs," but orbs of moist
clay. And the Grand Master does not
engage in intercourse with a silver-
haired matron, but rather with a young
blonde or redhead--one of the younger
Priory initiates to be sure. This younger
initiate who takes part in the Hieros
Gamos is selected by the Grand Master

during an earlier sacred ritual called *la Promenade de la Chatte.*

As for the Holy Grail, I will tell you about that too. *Rien ne se trouve si caché qui ne doive être connu.*

The Holy Grail is not some lost gospel or some descendant of a sacred bloodline like you read in *HBHG* or Dan Brown's book. Nothing of the sort. Instead it's a silver and gold chalice about five inches tall with a few of the precious gems missing from the rim. Though I saw photos of the Grail while in France, I didn't get to see the actual object until later in England, when I was made a *sénéchal.*

The late medieval design of the Grail chalice argues strongly against its having been used at the Last Supper. Any Priory member who believes this particular cup was used by Jesus of Nazareth is not likely to make it very far in the organization. Of course the Priory does not reject such initiates-- quite the contrary. Younger and more gullible Priory members are a necessary part of the organization, as can be seen above re: the Hieros Gamos. But the upper ranks--the *sénéchaux* of course and any of the approaching ranks--certainly these do not actually believe this object to date from ancient times.

As for the story of the sacred bloodline, it is one that predates Pierre Plantard--it is one of the only authentic Priory stories he maintains--but once again: Priory members consider this story a legend, a metaphor rather than history. Plantard himself was not a full Priory member. He came to the Priory as a clown and was allowed to set up shop with his greasepaint intact. But this in itself is a long story, one I will not go into here.

An interesting aside: The writer Dan Brown does seem to have at least a fleeting connection to the real modern history of the Priory, though I don't know where he got it. I knew Sophie Neveu when a student in Aix. She worked at the café on the Cours Mirabeau where most of us Priory members would meet for drinks. She even became a member eventually. She had long red hair just like in Brown's book. The last I saw her was in New York in 1998.

Now I've told you all the secrets I can tell you without really telling the secrets I can tell you. It's like with Strauss' *Persecution and the Art of Writing*. It's like with the purloined letter: sometimes the only safe place to hide things is out in the open. And what could be more out in the open than deadpan humor and ironic misdirection? Can you separate the one from the other? Can you find out the third?

If you're an attentive reader and have gotten this far, you can begin on a more diligent track by reading the following:

M_____ _____

An Isle of Rubble where ends a freeman's court,

Inscribed as Adam half my clues consort.

The title to this couplet, you see, is missing. If you want the title, you must figure it out from the clues available. Kind of like in the book. If you can't figure it out, just send a check for $199.79, made out to me, to

Eric Mader

c/o Z.E.I.

[*Address has changed.*

For current address,

query by email.]

Z.E.I. will get me your letter. They may be slow about it, but they will get it to me. And for your pains I will send you the title. But be warned: If you get the title and finally solve the couplet, then your real difficulties will begin. Which should be no surprise. It isn't easy being a knight. And what did you expect? To read a pulp thriller and be given the Keys to the Kingdom?

Eric Mader

Grand Master of the Priory of Sion

01/17/19

Eric Mader's Second Declaration

Why do you come here, reader? Do you expect to find another review of *The Da Vinci Code*? The hassle and hubbub that book has brought us, you can't imagine. Perhaps you expect to read here once again that Brown's book is an accomplished thriller, but that the author got half his historical facts wrong and sketched out a huge and absurd conspiracy where none was to be found. Is this what you're looking for? How many articles and books have gone over this same ground? Or is it maybe a movie review you expect?

In any case reviews are not what I'm going to offer. What I will write here is far more momentous. I'm going to uncover a secret in the real world--a secret I've kept for years but have finally tired of keeping. With this brief declaration I intend to tell the truth as it is. And so. . . .

I am the Grand Master of the Priory of Sion.

There--I've come out with it. You may have a hard time believing me, but your skepticism won't change the fact. I am the current Grand Master of the Priory and have been so for nearly a decade.

The truth is I've intended to tell about the Priory ever since they inducted me as an undergraduate. I first encountered and joined the Priory during my junior year abroad in France. That was in the late 1980s. But regardless of my ideas on what Priory secrecy ought to be and on how it should work in the organization, they insisted I not think of reform but should rather keep my mouth shut, both there at the meeting house off the Rue de la Violette in Aix, and then back in the States as I finished my degree and moved up the ranks. I was a newcomer after all, and as such I was persuaded to keep quiet and was even threatened.

"It's an ancient secret we protect," they'd tell me. "Any breach of the secret by a member will be punished with expulsion--or worse."

Back there in Aix and during the years following I had no choice but to listen. Besides which, there was some justice in their point, as my ideas would have meant a quite radical change in the organization as it related to the outside. Still, even then I suspected the worst punishment those pseudo-aristocrats could dole out would be forcing me to reread their "mystical" poems. But that generation of the Priory is now gone. Now that I am Grand Master, I intend to reform according to my original plans. Of the three *sénéchaux*, I know that two are in agreement with me. This declaration is the first step.

The Grand Master is I. I'm the man that leads the Priory. You wouldn't know it on the surface--actually I hold down a pretty normal job--but then that's just how it should be. We've always insisted on discretion, and will continue to do so, albeit in a different way.

But enough of my own story. My personal history is not my purpose here. There are other issues that need to be addressed, and I will first get to some of the more tiresome ones. I mean the questions that keep people up at night reading guides to Dan Brown's book--as if a thriller needs a guide!--those questions animating dinner parties and echoing round chat rooms. And so: *Is there reason to believe that Mary Magdalene was the wife of Jesus Christ? Did the Knights Templar uncover the Temple Treasure in Jerusalem at the time of the First Crusade? Do we Priory members really worship the sacred feminine and engage in ritual sex? Do we know where the Holy Grail is? Is there a "sacred bloodline" running from Jesus through the Merovingian kings and Pierre Plantard?*

Many of these questions are in fact laughable, and do not really relate to the Priory in any case.

As for Mary Magdalene and Jesus, the truth is that not even I, the Grand Master, can tell you reliably about that. And the reason is simple. The Priory of Sion doesn't go back that far, nor did our founders (rest their maligned souls) ever come upon any secret gospels relative to this question or any Temple Treasure either. So you will have to go to scholars if you want answers about Mary Magdalene--you will have to rest content with informed speculation, because nobody has concrete answers. And what did you expect?

As for the ritual sex, that part of Brown's book is mostly true, at least in terms of the Hieros Gamos being part of Priory tradition. Brown's presentation of the ritual is not quite correct however. During the Hieros Gamos the dancers do not hold "golden orbs," but orbs of moist clay. And the Grand Master does not engage in intercourse with any silver-haired matron, but rather with one of the younger Priory initiates, selected during an earlier Priory ritual by the body of participants.

I will tell you about the Holy Grail too, at least in terms of the material Grail, the Grail as object.

The Holy Grail is not Mary Magdalene or some cryptic scion of the Lord like you read in *Holy Blood, Holy Grail* or Brown's book. Nothing of the sort. Instead it's a silver and gold chalice about five inches tall with a few of the precious gems missing from the rim. Though I saw photos of the Grail while in France, I didn't see the actual object until later in England, when I was made a *sénéchal*.

The Grail chalice is indeed a symbolic object that holds its place in our doctrine and ritual. I am certain that this object in our possession has a history of many hundreds of years.

That said, some things become obvious to some, but need to be pointed out to others. The late medieval design of the Grail chalice held by the Priory argues strongly against its having been used at the Last Supper. Certainly no established Priory members actually believe this object dates from ancient times.

And so: the Holy Grail remains an idea, a focus of faith. The object held by the

Priory of Sion is a late medieval work of art and a part of certain of our rituals.

Given what has been said above regarding Mary Magdalene, it should be clear that the story of the sacred bloodline running through the Merovingians cannot be verified. Nonetheless this story certainly does predate Pierre Plantard. But once again: Priory members consider the story a legend, a metaphor rather than actual history.

Pierre Plantard himself was not a full Priory of Sion member. He came to the Priory as a clown and was allowed to set up shop with his greasepaint intact. The Priory encouraged him into action with the idea that he would do just what he did: discredit the Priory. Word of the actual organization had sparked too much interest among people the Priory wanted nothing to do with: anti-Semitic cranks, leftovers of the Vichy intelligentsia. There were people with clout that the Priory wanted to keep out, people pressing to find out more, to become members. One of the current *sénéchaux* was responsible for rumors of the Priory making the rounds in this group. Though his indiscretions ultimately led to his being demoted, the damage had already been done. The growing interest of these new would-be members--this and their correct suppositions as to the identity of various high-ranking Priory figures-- had to be diverted with a ruse. And so Plantard was brought in. He was encouraged to develop a cell of the Priory according to his own ideas, among which was the assertion that any viable spiritual organization needed to seek power in the political realm as well: that a political wing was necessary to continue the Priory's work. Of course it was suspected, given his character and concerns, that Plantard would soon be turning this new Priory cell into his own mythomaniacal fiefdom. In fact this is just what was wanted. His plans for maintaining the Priory's secret character while at the same time gaining new members were insincerely applauded by the actual Priory members he knew. The idea to claim his branch was named after the Mont Sion in Haute-Savoie was Plantard's. Although much of Plantard's correspondence hasn't been saved, the proud letter in which he announces this plan is still in the Priory archives.

Plantard was dealt with according to schedule. Eventually his Priory connections claimed the original organization was going defunct, that in fact his branch was the more vibrant and what was still held by the Priory would be transferred to him later. This was told to the busybodies too. For years they had taken Plantard as their connection, and it had been hinted to them that he was the man to watch. Then, finally, he was cut loose: the Priory didn't communicate with him any more.

Many of the best-known stories relating to the Priory come straight from Plantard and his desire for self-aggrandizement. Though the story of a sacred bloodline in Europe is part of Priory lore, in fact it is not a bloodline the Priory protects but a text and the teachings in that text. Or rather: It is not an actual bloodline we protect but a text and the teachings embodied in that text.

An interesting aside: The writer Dan Brown does seem to have at least a fleeting connection to the real modern history of the Priory, though I don't know where he got it. I knew Sophie Neveu when a student in Aix. She worked at the café on the Cours Mirabeau where most of us Priory members would meet for drinks. She even became a member eventually. She had long red hair just like in Brown's book. The last I saw her was in New York in 1998.

Now I've told you all the secrets I can tell you without really telling the secrets I can tell you. It's like with Strauss' *Persecution and the Art of Writing*. It's like with the purloined letter: sometimes the only safe place to hide things is out in the open. And what could be more out in the open than this declaration? Can you separate the Priory from the myriad fictions it has spawned? Can you find out the third?

If you're an attentive reader and have gotten this far, you can begin on a more diligent track by reading the following:

M_____ _____

Where Harvey stopp'd there rises Babel's Doom,

Its mossy stones a Ziggurat entomb.

Where he left off, there seek our scattered Keys;

The Doors to open up in just degrees.

The title, as you see, poem is missing. You must figure it out from the clues available. This, I know, is rather like in the book: that world-shaking thriller in which most people first learned of the Priory. But be warned: If you get the title and finally interpret my poem, then your real difficulties begin. Which should be no surprise. It isn't easy being a knight, not

even in this belated age. And what did
you expect? To find [   ] revealed in
pulp thrillers and pseudo-histories?

Eric Mader

Grand Master of the Priory of Sion

01/17/19

"Risks of Decoding Priory of Sion Internal Correspondence"

Note: This response can be found at
http://www.claytestament.blogspot.com

Some weeks ago a young Irish friend of mine named Paul Wylie posted the following photo on Facebook. (A photograph of Coco Chanel and Jean Cocteau) He didn't know then that figures quite like these, with less talent however, were at that very moment looming just on the periphery of his humdrum student life, threatening to move in and suffocate him in the rosy flower of youth.

For Paul Wylie had gotten involved in a plot to decode the several parts of the Internal Correspondence of the Priory of Sion that had so far been made public. It was his acquaintance with one S. Owens that brought him too close to the Priory to allow him ever to be completely free of it again. What started as a bit of historical sleuthing for one curious Irish university student was turning into something else entirely.

Yesterday evening I noticed Mr. Wylie clamouring for my attention in chat, as if I didn't have enough on my hands already with the recent leak of Priory documents:

Paul: Hey Eric, can I reproduce the coded Priory Correspondence in book format? For my private use only. I'd appreciate it very much. I should add, both coded and decoded, Vols. I & II.

Eric: Certainly, Paul. We will not cause you any trouble. ;)

Paul: Thanks, I knew you wouldn't object! ;) – I felt as though I had to do the winky face back. Y'know, because you did it. But you did it in an ambiguous way. Some burly men aren't going to come and kidnap me are they? They won't have their way with a delicate soul like me? Will they? Although that could be fun.

Eric: On the outside we do not look burly. But don't misunderestimate us. We are deadly. In order to protect what we protect, which is the thing we hold

under our protection, we will shrink
from no deadpan intervention, no
matter how unpleasant, that might
prove necessary.

On the outside we look like Jean
Cocteau, or even like Coco Chanel. But
on the inside we are not what we seem.
We are something else. From what we
seem, that is. On the inside, that is.
Because you shouldn't be fooled by the
outside, which is a different side
altogether. Still, the outside can be
pretty snotty on its own if needs be. Say,
for instance, the inside is busy
contemplating Priory business, and the
outside, looking like Jean Cocteau or
Coco Chanel, feels a looming threat. It
may simply, the outside I mean, NOT
EVEN INFORM the inside of said
threat, but decide to handle it on its
own. And you don't want to see it. You
think French waiters are snotty? Hah.
Don't make me laugh. THAT is not
snotty by Priory standards.

So it is not the burly fellows you need to
worry about, Wylie. By publicizing

internal Priory documents you are moving to an entirely different level of danger here. Never forget that the root word of "deadpan" is "dead". And "pan". Never forget that, Wylie.

You may share these words with Ms. Owens if you like. We know her role in the decoding. She has won a place in our hearts by naming a lamb after us. It is a deeply archetypal gesture. But we have our limits. We do have our limits, Wylie.

Paul: What if I name a dog after you?

Eric: This is an archetype that, I'm sure you are aware, could point different ways. If you were to name a Chihuahua after me, for instance, you would be putting yourself in serious danger. Imagine Jean Cocteau and Coco Chanel X 1000. So choose your dog wisely, Wylie.

Paul: A Scotch terrier mutt?

Eric: I'm going against my better judgment here, but will conclude by saying: Don't inform Ms. Owens of this brief chat. Tomorrow I will make a more public warning. I think others may benefit from this too. There are, after all, untold numbers of Chihuahuas out there, unnamed and threatening. So tomorrow you and Ms. Owens will be cited in a public manner. Until then, make no mention to her.

S. Owens: Eric, I named one of our pedigree Texel lambs after you. Here we go, Eric the lamb!

*

Yes, it was a wonderful gesture on Ms. Owens' part. She had been made aware of all the people her rash revelations had put at risk, and was trying by this to apologize to me personally, the current Grand Master. I was appeased. The lamb is surpassing cute after all. And previously I'd never had anything named after me except a half a bee.

And so: For the time being, Paul and Shonie, I will think of the lamb when I think of this unfortunate leak of internal Priory documents. In other words, I will think of myself. For I am pedigree and warm of aspect, not snotty like my minions who, at this very moment, are waiting to pounce. They have heard word that the Priory has been compromised, and they await orders to act. They wait in chic cafes and hotel lobbies, waiting for my word, the word that will send them out with withering snottiness, a snottiness of such chic ferocity as to discomfit and ruin the lives of any they might glom onto. Yes, they are eager to train this deadpan snottiness on those who have compromised Priory secrets.

For now, however, I am thinking of the lamb, and so I will let it pass. They will sit in those cafes and hotel lobbies and run up big tabs with the sullen waiting, tabs that will be on us to cover, but I am thinking of the lamb, so I will cover their tabs.

Any others in fair Ireland or elsewhere who would divulge Priory secrets should think on Jean Cocteau and Coco Chanel instead--rather, they should imagine slightly smaller but snottier

versions, whole troupes of Jeans and Cocos, swarming about you with dry remarks and cold gazes. And then you will have nowhere to hide. And then there will be no lamb cute enough to thwart my certain vengeance.
Eric Mader,

G.M.P.o.S.

"This young Irish fellow is going to be the end of us."

Note: This message can be found at http://www.claytestament.blogspot.com

…Or, as I see it, he may become part of the new beginning I have in mind.

I know three or four of you who read this don't agree with me here, and think besides that my prevarications serve no purpose. But as I've explained to you before, in weightier correspondence, my purpose is clear enough for me: it's simply a long way down the road.

So the prevarication will have to go on.

Young Wylie and his mysterious female accomplice have cracked the ciphers of the posted Internal Correspondence . The deciphered texts, most of them, have now been published in book form. Today I'm posting this to give them my congratulations.

What worries me slightly, at this point,

is that Wylie may figure out what is serious in my initial announcement, and that if he does, he will insist on divulging what he finds. I say it worries me slightly; I know it worries some of you quite a bit. In fact I don't think there's much danger on either score: 1) that he will figure it out; 2) that he would divulge anything without warrant. Either way, you four will have to put up with the slight jeopardy you see.

He's very young, yes, but we need youth, no? We're old; getting too old for our own good.

He's very young, yes, but I think he's playing for the long game. He didn't publish Letter 17 after all.

So congratulations, Wylie. I'm hoping your name turns out to indicate what I think it does.

For you others, who dissent, I know I'll be hearing from you soon. As always, I'll listen carefully to any concerns you

have. I'm confident you'll see eventually
that my reasoning on these issues is
sound.

From game to gunm,
From dog to doggerel,
Yours truly,

Eric Mader,

G.M.P.o.S.

"Confession of a Seneschal."

I was surfing the web a few weeks ago
and came across a mysterious
declaration from a man who claimed to
be the Grand Master of the even-more-
mysterious-than-he secret organisation
known as The Priory of Sion. His name,
I saw, was Eric Mader-Lin. Having read
his declaration I decided that I believed
him and his claim to Grand Mastership
of the Priory. At the end of the
declaration was a link to "The Priory
Documents: *Internal Correspondence of the
Priory of Sion*". The sight of the encoded
documents excited me as much as the
next 19-year-old Psychology student
with an interest in codes. I printed the
documents and sat down with a pen to
try and crack the code. And what, I hear
you ask, was the reward for my efforts?
Discussion about books between Eric
Mader-Lin and D.M.S.
Then...*disaster.* The code changed! No
longer could I consult the key - No
longer could I find solace in
reading *another* message about books
and Dan Brown-esque Priory nonsense.
I was lost! Darkness swept over the

bright lights of my enlightenment, and my soul died.

Eventually I recovered from my melodramatic depression and set about cracking the new code, which I eventually did. I continued decoding the last bulk of the document, but took the precaution of working solely from my computer. I worked out that it was easier to have the new key and encoded documents side-by-side on a computer screen than on flammable paper. Finally, the finish line was in sight! I had three pages left to decode...and...*DISASTER*. My soul, like a phoenix, or a trite simile, had been reincarnated only to be cast down into the dark and fiery chasm from whence it came.

The cause of this second and doubly devastating disaster was a computer virus. I had been working in the University library the previous night, and evidently had downloaded a virus on to my USB memory stick. Not only did I lose the bulk of decoded Priory documents, but I also lost several essays due the following week. I panicked. What would I do? All of mine and S's hard work for naught! - I sought the help of the Grand Master. In a grand and masterful way I brown nosed him, massaged his (surprisingly tense) ~~shoulders~~ ego and explained the situation to him. I asked him if he, to spare me *a lot* of extra work to which I couldn't lend any time, could get me the key for the messages that had been lost to the computer virus. He being a Grand Master of courtesy granted my request under several conditions. This blog is one of those conditions.

I'm still waiting for the key, but then, I haven't fulfilled my side of the bargain yet. I haven't, as I have been instructed, procured for his use a box of matches and 100 copies of Dan Brown's *The Da Vinci Code*. I am confident that when I have fulfilled that most solemn of promises, I will be able to move forward with publishing the Priory documents so that all the world might enjoy a slice of de-mystified mystery.

I like this business of blog writing. It's cathartic. Not as cathartic as seeing a well-done production of *King Lear*, but quite a bit more cathartic than relieving oneself of mass amounts of excrement after a long day of holding it in. I know what you're thinking: this whole blog entry has been a mass amount of excrement. O give me a break. I'm a weathered, experienced and devoted seneschal in the Priory of Sion. I have seen things, done things, heard things and said things that you will never know! Not that you'd want to. . . Curiosity and cats, eh?

Your friend,

P.W., P.o.S.

"A Message to my Priory peers."

I've been a member of the P.o.S. for a few months now. I've tried to be as productive as I can in that time: I've published a Priory-related book and I've done a few other assignments related to my training.

I'm idle at the moment, hence this blog post, but I hope to be on another assignment soon. The purpose of this post is to officially declare my allegiance to the organisation.

I understand that some of my peers within the Priory disagree with me being so quickly promoted to the rank I now have. I don't blame them: I'm much younger than many of them, I'm inexperienced and I'm still learning exactly what the Priory's aims are. If any of you, my peers, are reading this, I would ask for your patience and tolerance as I make my way through my training. I hope to meet many of you in the near future, and I hope that I'll prove to be a valuable asset to the organisation.

THE PRIORY
DOCUMENTS

Letter 1: A letter from D.M.S. to E.M. regarding the latter's revelations at PRIORY

BABYLON:

From: D.M.S. ----- s--------@yahoo.com

To: Eric Mader, inthemargins03@hotmail.com

Subject: re: Sangreal

Date: Sun, 28th Nov 2004 04:03:54 +0000 (GMT)

Eric,

I'd long suspected it. But are you really part of the great line of Priory leaders? They were all gay and were direct descendants of Jesus. Therefore, Parthenogenesis continues unabated to this day. Debussy is Jesus! And when you listen to La Mer it is really about Ma Mere.

D.M.S.

Letter 2: E.M. replies to D.M.S.

D.M.S.:

Yes! You are starting to understand. Debussy is a direct descendant of Jesus through parthenogenesis affected by his mother. This is a sacred mystery. Jean Cocteau is a direct descendant of Coco Chanel in the same way, as hinted in the recent Chanel commercial featuring Nicole Kidman. Kidman, I'm sure you know, has links to the same Scotch family, the Sinclairs, that gave us Rosslyn Chapel and Bowmore single malt. And golf. I see by your mention of La Mer that you're beginning to realise your own place in all this. The plot finally comes full circle. Your mother turned 98 in 2004 in the 11th month. The numbers work out perfectly. I will make you a seneschal upon your return to Taipei.

G.M.

Letter 3: D.M.S. to E.M.

Dear G.M.,

If you're ever browsing the National Library for a good book, and one with relevance to your status as Grand Master, you might search for this one: Paul Waley. TOKYO NOW AND THEN (New York and Tokyo: Weatherhill, 1984 ISBN 0-8348-0195-7)

This is probably the best English book ever written about an Asian capital, comparable to the recent LONDON: A BIOGRAPHY by whatsisname--Peter Ackroyd, or was it Dan Ackroyd

Paul Waley was an old Tokyo drinking buddy of mine (i.e, we once drank a little too much sake together) and worked with me at Kodansha. He is the grandnephew of Arthur Waley, the bizarre first translator of the tales of GENJI, who apparently taught himself Japanese and never spoke a word himself. Waley and I appear to be distantly related to each other through the family of Siegried Sassoon, the former Jewish bankers to the Caliph of

Baghdad, who intermarried with Strouds and Waleys when they reached England. Which makes me an Iraqi.

Anyway, to make a long dog story short, on pp. 60-61, you will find a discussion of the greatest work of Takizawa Bakin, a major Edo period writer. It is called BIOGRAPHIES OF EIGHT DOGS, which was published in 106 volumes. It tells "the story of eight heroes born of a mystical union between a valiant dog and the daughter of the first Satomi lord of the province of AWA" (modern Chiba Prefecture).

Your Devout Seneschal

Letter 4: E.M. to D.M.S.

With a scholarly persistence worthy of Dan Brown himself, I've checked out these new claims of yours and am now able to ask--Devout Senechal you call yourself? Bah! If it's true as you say that you are descended via parthenogenesis from Vidal Sassoon and that you were in Baghdad when it was stormed by the Samurai Dogs as we read in the epic EIGHT AGAINST BAGHDAD--if this is true, then you my friend, and not me or even Jean Cocteau's literary executor, must be the REAL Grand Master of the Priory.

What a fool I was not to see it! All along I thought Ma Mere was La Mer, but here it turns out that your Mere is. I suppose you've just been humoring me, watching me make a fool of myself, showing me that fake Grail in London and waiting for me to announce myself to all the world. But I'm not so naive as you might think. For one, I've read a lot of Bakhtin myself, even a biography. I just never knew he wrote on the EIGHT AGAINST BAGHDAD. I will certainly check out Dan Ackroyd's book on London.

Former G.M.,

Now Loyal Seneschal,

E.M.

Letter 5: D.M.S. to E.M.

Dear Former GM,

Buried directly under the keystone at St. Sulpice, you will find a casket containing the secret name of Baghdad, which is:

DOG BAGGED.

The secondary transcription is:

DAG BAG IT.

Hope you have read the key passage in Cortazar's RAYUELA (HOPSCOTCH) about St. Sulpice and the hit and run accident on the Rue Madame. I was there. I suffered. I died.

New Grand Master.

Letter 6: E.M. to D.M.S.:

Dang bad. I've already admitted that you are probably the Grand Master, but here you are, still fooling with me as if I was born yesterday. I know very well that the secret name of Baghdad is NOT in a casket in St. Sulpice, and I know this because of course I read the part in the novel where Silas finds the casket and there is a scrap of paper in it with the biblical verse. So I'm not going to be fooled by your fiction when Brown's novel tells the truth for all the world to see.

As for HOPSCOTCH, the author should have stuck with good plotting procedures and not mixed everything up like he did. Even Priory members like Cortazar need to stick to the rules of good fiction, don't you think? I mean, you'll never see a major motion picture starring Tom Hanks coming out of HOPSCOTCH. And there's indication Cortazar himself saw the novel wasn't as good as Dan Brown's books. Because if you analyse the title you see what it's really all about. HOPSCOTCH being

HOP SCOTCH, which is Scotch made from hops, which is as they used to say in the Renaissance--small beer.

And stop it with the dog jokes already! My Louis in A TAIPEI MUTT may not be descended from any of those eight Samurai Dogs that harried Baghdad, but still his pedigree is not something to be sneezed at. Louis, a SCOTCH terrier mutt--I'm sure you noticed that, didn't you?--was descended parthenogenetically from Apuleius' Lucius. I was in fact reading Apuleius when the conception occurred. Now Apuleius' Lucius was an ass, I admit it, but still he was no ordinary ass, but a GOLDEN ASS, one more that Thomas Aquinas went out of his way to naysay as being mere fiction. And when Thomas Aquinas himself has to insist that something is mere fiction. you know it must be the opposite: it must be REAL.

E.M.,

Senechal, PoS

P.S.--But I remember also the moment of Louis' parthenogenic conception, a moment fraught with significance. Consider: I was working at the time at the Hua Language Institute here in Taipei. Of course you're aware that the Chinese character "Hua" in the institute's name means "flower"--Hua being the surname of the man who founded the institute. Presently the Hua Institute has almost two dozen branches in Taipei, and you might wonder at which branch I was working. Well, it was the branch on Roosevelt Road, on the corner of Ho-Ping E. Road and Roosevelt Road to be exact. Of course Roosevelt Road is not just named after the American president. Roosevelt in Dutch, etymologically that is, means "Rose Field" and Roosevelt Road is laid on the ancient Rose Line of Formosa, a line that bisects the island down the middle and extends underwater up through China. The ancient Shang capital was in fact recently proven to have been built on the northern end of this line, ineluctably linking the island of Formosa with the Chinese, regardless of what the DPP and the pro-independence crowd might think.

So my Louis was parthenogenetically conceived in a fifth floor office situated on the Rose Line of Asia. And as if to stress this fact the conception occurred precisely in the office of the Hua Language Institute, "Hua" in Chinese meaning "Flower."

But that is not all. Did you notice the cross street of that intersection on which my office was located? Did you note it? I'm sure you did. It is none other than Ho-Ping East Road, "HoPing" meaning "Peace." My interpretation of this is as follows: On the Rose Line of Asia, Louis Kemp was conceived, a literary character, a man turned mutt, a man destined to bring peace to Asia if only his rightful place is recognized.

I still await a good Chinese translation of the book, and then the New Era for Asia can begin.

Letter 7: E.M. to D.M.S.

G.M. Shroud:

I've got orders for two of L's books and for two of Donald Richard's: around one hundred books altogether. I just talked with him on the phone and he has directed me to Stone Bridge.

I'm still waiting for Bookman to respond on the RC Allen books. Their manager has changed. I've received all of the copies of CAUGHT IN THE ACT you sent, and will try to get homes for them.

E.M. (Former G.M.)

P.S.--Though I write you today of L., Allen and Richie, this book dealer's talk should not lead you to think that I've forgotten our differences. No, I have not forgotten. The Priory and its work are in my thoughts day and night. It is on this score, in fact, that I add this postscript. I want you to know that I have found vindication; that I have found a champion and your dog jokes can touch me no more.

Do you know who wrote me today? I will let you guess--No, you're wrong. In fact it is Dr. Barbara Gray who has written me. Yes, THE Dr. Barbara Gray. You don't believe it? But I've got THE letter right here. It seems Dr. Gray read the text in which I declined for all the world my (now willingly abdicated) Priory Grand Mastership. It seems that the contents of the text stirred in her certain psychic energies, which called forth in her certain certainties. Of this at least I am certain. Feeling the pull of etheric certainty, Dr. Gray felt compelled to contact me about my claims. Her letter--I have it right here-- goes as follows:

Dear Eric:

I invite you to visit my web page. There are some new things there which you must see. I feel you are of the Knights in a past life.

Sincerely,

Dr Barbara Gray.

The importance of such a letter, coming from Barbara Gray, should be obvious. Though I'm confident you already know her work--even a Grand Master has much to learn from a woman like Barbara Gray--I will quote from the self-introduction she offers on her web page. Perhaps this self-introduction will remind you of some of Dr. Gray's accomplishments:

BARBARA GRAY

Barbara Gray has lived and studied Christian Mysticism for thirty years. To help her achieve her destiny and gift to earth, she experienced external Apparitions of Light Figures since childhood. Her mind-consciousness education began with pre-medicine, branched into psychology, the study of altered states of consciousness, parapsychology, parapsychology and medicine, world religions and the psychology of social change. To better prepare her for her destiny, during and prior to her post-graduate education, she gained experience in missile systems technology, the medical field and oceanographic field.

After achieving her higher degrees, she set about in 1977 on a twenty-six-year walk-about to educate the public about its true purpose in life, the evolution of its spiritual nature and its Divination. She introduced to scientists, clergymen, teachers, and medical researchers, inner spiritual techniques to advance their creative nature. In her twenty years on the road, she has appeared on many radio and television interviews, a guest speaker at Universities, and general public lectures. In all instances possible, she transferred her audience into the Heaven Realm for an Objective Reality to their Higher Self/Holy Spirit, Christ, and God.

Probably much of this is familiar to you. In any event, the letter from Dr. Gray is vindication from an authority, Master Shroud. An expert in parapsychology and oceanography, Gray has an undeniable connection to the Spiritual Realm. If she didn't, how could she have had the Apparitions of Light Figures? Tell me that. Nobody without a connection to the Spiritual Realm can ever hope to have Apparitions of Light Figures--I think we can all agree.

I may not be Grand Master now, Dr. Gray seems to be saying, but I must have been in a previous life. This at least is how I interpret her letter. So it seems your place is not as secure as you thought. A former Grand Master can always re-incarnate, especially since I'm already alive. Don't get me wrong, Shroud. I don't hope for schism in the Priory. We must continue to work as one. But on the other hand, I insist on a certain respect. I'm sure you noticed that Dr. Gray also studied missile systems technology. In terms of modern missile technology, San Francisco is not all that far from Taipei, and I do have your address there. Keep these facts in mind next time you try to fool me with nonsense about the secret names of Baghdad.

Letter 8: E.M. to D.M.S.

G.M.:

Peter Goodman has contacted me about the Richie order, in brief that it will fall through, and I wrote back to let him know that in any case I could help get the order to their distributor. I'm just not sure Eslite would agree to the terms, or that their distributor will be able to really communicate with Eslite, being that my main contact speaks only Chinese. Maybe as middleman I could eventually cut a profit to buy a tomato juice at the 7-Eleven. It's okay either way. I know my big profits in terms of books will only come when you finish the Spanish translation of A TAIPEI MUTT and Garcia Marquez writes that introduction he promised championing the "new Formosan magical Realism." Yes, it was easier to make money when we Knights Templar financed Kings.

Eric

Letter 9: D.M.S. to E.M.

Senechal Mader:

Let's hope Barbara Gray is a Labyrinth Walker too. Perhaps Peter Goodman at Stone Bridge can give you some compensation for snagging those orders. You think I don't give you enough respect? But I've just recently given the MUTT a new SARU ISBN: 0-935086-29-3.

The copies have here will all get decorated with new little (barking) seals.

Letter 10: E.M. to D.M.S.

"Now flam'd the Dog Star's unpropitious ray,

Smote ev'ry brain, and wither'd every bay;

Sick was the sun, the owl forsook his bow'r.

The moon-struck prophet felt the madding hour:

Then rose the seed of Chaos, and of Night,

To blot out order, and extinguish light,

Of dull and venal a new world to mould,

And bring Saturnian days of lead and gold."

--*Alexander Pope: Dunciad IV*

Master Shroud:

A new letter has come to me from Dr. Gray. It confirms what I suspected. In fact I AM the Grand Master and you are not. The letter is as follows:

Dear Eric:

Thank you for your kind letter. I write you with some tidings. An apparition of light appeared to me this afternoon, a strong one with many colours. Among the colours was a dog dressed all in white, a terrier, his clothes shining like the sun. I fell to my knees on the grass. I was walking my own dog in the park at the time, which I do usually in the afternoons. This time my dog ran away because of the apparition! The terrier approached me and put a paw on my shoulder. Then it said in a clear and thundering voice: "The rightful Grand Master of the

Priory will write to you under the sign of the Dog." And suddenly it was gone.

Well I went to find my collie then and finally I found her. She was so scared by the apparition she was off hiding in the A&E parking lot.

I called the terrier apparition "The Dog of Thunder" and I am painting it now on one of my apparition cards.

I remember that you wrote me about your novel, A TAIPEI MUTT, and how it was about a dog. So the Grand Master must be

you because nobody else who was formerly
of the Knights as I could sense in my
spiritual vision has also written to me about
a dog.

Congratulations! What will be your first
action as Grand Master?

Dr. Barbara Gray

Regardless of your insubordination, I
feel the Priory still needs good men like
you, so I will still be willing to make
you a seneschal upon your arrival in
Taipei. I much appreciate your efforts
on behalf of the Dog in the U.S. and see
very well the geometric significance of
the new ISBN number.

In cano veritas,

G.M.

'Tis true, on words is still our whole debate,

Disputes of Me or Te , of aut or at,

To sound or sink in cano ,

O or A, Or give up Cicero to C or K.

Let Friend affect to speak as Terence spoke,

And Alsop never but like Horace joke:

For me, what Virgil, Pliny may deny,

Manilius or Solinus shall supply:

For Attic Phrase in Plato let them seek,

I poach in Suidas for unlicens'd Greek.

In ancient sense if any needs will deal,

Be sure I give them fragments, not a meal. .
."

- Ibid.

Letter 11: D.M.S. to E.M.

Dear Grand Master (Restored):

Your arguments are irrefutable as they are insufferable. Yes, I can suffer it no more and I freely admit my insubordination to your rightful rule of the Priory. I look forward to being made a seneschal upon my return to Taipei. Will the ceremony take place at the intersection of Eastern Peace with the north-south Rose Line?

D.M.S.

(Defrocked G.M. of the PoS)

Letter 12: "L.D.O." to E.M.

From: "N/A N/A" g--------
@hotmail.com

To: inthemargins03@hotmail.com

Subject: Membership Request

Date: Wed, 08, Dec. 2004 22:17:17 +0200

Dear Great Master,

I would like to become a member of the Priory of Sion. Especially as a senechaux.

How can I be admitted to this great organisation?

I look forward to hearing from you.

With respect,

Leonardo De Ouchy

Letter 13: E.M. to "L.D.O."

Dear Mr. De Ouchy:

You are already a member of the Priory. As per a resolution we adopted in 1997, anyone who desires to become a member of the Priory of Sion becomes a member the moment such desire is present. In other words: desire to join the Priory is to join the Priory.

As for our teachings, that is a different matter. Many members know little or nothing of our teachings because they make no effort to discover those teachings. Dan Brown's extreme distortion of Priory doctrine in his novel has only exacerbated this ignorance regarding what the Priory is, what it keeps alive in terms of tradition. But we will not bemoan this situation. The distance between the misconceptions held by Priory members and our actual teachings doesn't much trouble us.

As for you becoming a seneschal, you shouldn't even think of it. For one thing you don't even know enough about the rank of seneschal to see that senechaux is the plural form of the word. And so at present you've about as much chance of becoming a geese as you do of becoming a senechaux. Probably even more chance.

Sincerely,

E.M.

Letter 14: E.M. to D.M.S.

Dear Shroud:

Just received the following.

****

Re: New Information from the Knights
Templar Inner Circle

Here is some information which today
was made available online on a new
website:

1.   In 44 A.D. Jesus kissed Mary
Magdalene and their children goodbye
as he stayed in the Middle East, while
Mary, Tamar, Jesus the younger and
Joseph went to Gaul, or southern
France.

2.   If the spiritual teacher of Joan of
Arc had stopped teaching after Joan was
burned alive, who would have taught
Leonardo da Vinci?

3.   In 1128 A.D., the inner circle of
the Knights Templar returned to France
with the Ark, and Stones, of the
Covenant, priceless documents and

Jesus' artifacts, like his and Mary's red crystal Wedding Chalice.

The writings on this new website include information about the secret travels of Jesus to England and India, his survival of the crucifixion, Mary Magdalene's royal heritage, their children and the Knights Templar's Inner Circle.

The site is a gift to humanity from the Protectors of the Holy Grail, a secret hereditary organisation which has decided to release some private information about The True Jesus, his wife and children.

In the 21st Century, direct descendants of the Inner Circle of the Knights Templar in the Americas, Europe, the Middle East, Africa and elsewhere began awakening their ancestral memories. This DNA awakening process of the descendants was made possible by the information of Cee-Jus, the last of their Great Grand Masters of the Knights Templar Inner Circle.

And so it was that one Inner Circle descendant went into isolation in 2001 to focus on the Cee-Jus information. In this manner, the ancient techniques of Cee-Jus were recovered. Then, the one became the many, by his teaching other descendants. In 2004, after several years of working with portions of the techniques, the parts were brought together, and thus the many became the one.

The writings of Cee-Jus, last Great Grand Master of the Knights Templar Inner Circle, are now being released to all people in the world for free. The website is at

www.TheTrueJesus.org

Enjoy,

Katy Firenze

****

None of this is very significant, but I still think our brothers over at the Temple shouldn't be putting it on the web. Anyhow, I used to drink Cee-Jus when I was a student in France. Even before joining the Priory.

There are things in this information I don't quite trust. For one, this talk of Jesus and Mary's "red crystal Wedding Chalice." I've seen pieces of their Aramaic bone china, but I've never heard of any wedding chalice.

It's known that Mary and children went to Gaul because she'd wanted to go there for the honeymoon but Jesus insisted on taking a cruise in the Aegean. E.M. Illluminatus,

M.A.,

G.M. P.o.S.

Letter 15: D.M.S. to E.M.:

Dear Eric the Black:

Salutations on the 230th anniversary of the American Revolution, long may it wave. The new Emily Dickinson book SOLITARY PROWESS will be out on May 17th and will be followed by our commentary on the Templars, SOLITARY CHALICE.

The two Tanikawa books look beautiful and should be at the printers next week. I just rented a second apartment next door to my own to accommodate my mother and those thousands of new unsold books. I moved her from an apartment one block away which became infested with cockroaches.

They were attracted by the aura of my carefully hidden copy of the Grail, sculpted by Michelangelo while he was working on the Laocoon. He added wine residue from broken Roman bottles for authenticity.

Any word of SALES from Le Grand Eslite? Maybe we should have tried Geant or Carrefour instead. I did sell one more copy of MUTT at City Lights. Did you get L.'s books and did anyone review them? Looks like we will be having Eggs Benedict from now on.

Drieux

Letter 16: E.M. to D.M.S.

Dear Stroud:

It seems you are more concerned with the book trade than with your true Priory calling. What's more, you write in what seems to me a joking tone.

For your information, L.'s books have not yet been reviewed, but I suspect they will be sooner or later. And le Grand Eslite has sold at least two copies of HOMESICK FOR DEATH. I'm certain in any case they have sold two since the start of this year. I'd have to square accounts with them to figure out if more have been sold in total. And I square accounts with them about once a year.

"Bring out number weight and measure in a year of dearth."

If this is the kind of year you are in, let me know and I will start peddling DEATH on the sidewalks. Or peddling DEATH and APPEARANCES.

But how is it that you've nothing to say on the Oxyrhynchus finds? The Gospel fragment is sure to give Benedict indigestion. Or have you not read of the Gospel fragment yet? The find was written up in a recent issue of THE LIVERPOOL OBSERVER of all places. I found it so Prioresque that I posted it on my page:

http://www.necessaryprose.com/oxyrhynchus.htm

I only hope they don't find more of that particular Gospel. The Gaul narratives could lead straight to the Grotto of Merovee, and thence to the stele with the map to the crypt.

Think I ought to move them when I'm there in July? Or should I just get Guido to do it like last time?

Travailler toujours,

E.M.

SUPPLEMENTARY MATERIAL

*Interview with Nicolas Haywood,
spokesman for the Priory of Sion.*

B.B.: Are you a member of the Priory of Sion?

N.H.: I have friends in the Priory of Sion. I speak on their behalf. Sion is not really a secret organisation. Sion just does not choose to operate, and cannot operate, in the light. There is a lot to fear, in some respects. We do not seek publicity but we delight on occasion when the right people come along with the right mindset, and intention. And that is why I am here.

B.B.: Do you believe or does the Priory believe or have evidence that Jesus married Mary [Magdalene] and had children?

N.H.: Yes. Yes is the simple answer to that.

B.B.: Is there a bloodline of Jesus and Mary?

N.H.: There is a bloodline of Jesus and Mary, yes. There is.

B.B.: Do you have evidence within the Priory? Is there evidence?

N.H.: There is evidence beyond question… There exists evidence beyond question, but the mainstay of evidence itself is a series of items which are kept together, a series of objects. I will not go any further than that and explain what those objects are. They are unquestionable.

B.B.: Are they in the possession of the Priory?

N.H.: Their whereabouts is in the possession of the Priory.

B.B.: Did Mary Magdalene come to France?

N.H.: The *body* of evidence itself attests to that wholeheartedly.

B.B.: Is that in France?

N.H.: Yes.

B.B.: Who is the Priory, and specifically, what are its aims or raison d'être?

N.H.: Its aims are to protect and at the same time promulgate ancient truths, ancient mysteries. To say that they are protecting any *thing*, any one thing is difficult. They are protecting much more than one nameable secret... Or unnameable secret. Their ultimate goal is not one of world domination, but one of world unity and the evolution of man to the next rightful stage.

B.B.: Does it exist in the shadows? Is that where it's most comfortable?

N.H.: If you're in the shadows you have a clearer view of the light.

B.B.: I know one of the big questions that people have is, you know, journalists and authors have had a very hard time pinning down the Priory's true history in documentary form or historically, and that's cast a big shadow on the veracity of its being. How can you help us with that?

N.H.: Sion surfaces in a manner that allows it to be seen. It leaves its imprints a little like any traveller. It surfaces at times in history when it is expedient for it to make appearances, although they are in the general sense and time frame, fleeting. But it is a pre-Christian concept or ideal. It stretches back as old as man, I suppose. It takes many shapes and forms simply because it is forced to evolve and change its features and adjust in an ever-changing world which, indirectly, it aids the changing of. It plays its own part culturally.

B.B.: Is it possible, not now, for the Priory to prove, let's say beyond reasonable doubt its history and provenance and therefore its reality, or not?

N.H.: Ultimately, yes. But in doing that to the ultimate, to the final goal, it would facilitate showings its hand, as it were, which it's not yet prepared to do. But it will do. It doesn't *need* to do that, in all honesty. It never has needed to do that. And it is really not important that we're believed or not believed, at this point in time. There will come a time when much of what has been said that is correct, and much of what has been fathomed by others in whose steps you follow will be all too clear. I can't really elucidate any further on that. But we are comfortable with that. The fact that enquiring minds may not be so comfortable… It's not our problem, really.

B.B.: But categorically, it is a real Order?

N.H.: Yes.

B.B.: And it can trace its history back to pre-Christian times?

N.H.: Yes.

B.B.: What sort of people are members of the Priory today?

N.H.: All kinds of people. There are people from the world of literature, the world of the arts, in all forms. There are ecclesiastical members; members of the Church. There are individuals who are spiritually orientated, there are philosophically orientated individuals.

B.B.: Presumably you're approached to join?

N.H.: Yes.

B.B.: Do you have to be a Mason or is that not important?

N.H.: It's not important.

B.B.: How much can you tell us about the objects that you have, the physical evidence that you have and what form that takes?

N.H.: I'm not prepared to tell you anything about that. What I can tell you is that there is a body of evidence that exists.

B.B.: Incontrovertible?

N.H.: Incontrovertible.

B.B.: That if it was revealed would change mass opinion?

N.H.: That would depend on *when* it were revealed. As we reach a point in our evolution where the Church's role is increasingly less-and-less, and science revolves around and around in a nutshell of its own making learning more and more about less-and-less. It's about the timing. If it's timed correctly it shouldn't come as too much of a blow. In fact, it will become, "*Ah, probably, oh well it's just as we suspected.*" – That is the response that is hoped for.

B.B.: Can you see that body of evidence being revealed in my lifetime?

N.H.: Possibly. Quite possibly.

B.B.: Is there something coming? Is there an event? Is there a happening?

N.H.: Yes. There is an event. There is going to be something happening that nobody will be able to turn around and say, "*Oh, hang on, was that the event or have we still got to wait for it?*".

B.B.: In my lifetime?

N.H.: In your lifetime, yeah.

B.B.: Can you give us a theory as to what it is?

N.H.: I suppose it could be said that at this point in time the human race is gradually reaching a point of cessation of time itself. The seasons merge one into the next. It is a gradual cessation of time. And that cannot happen without the collapse of various other natural structures, structures inherent in the mechanics of nature itself. And we're already witnessing that. It is in-keeping with a much larger cycle.

B.B.: We're watching time slowing down?

N.H.: Dissolve, really. Yeah.

B.B.: Are we talking about a sort of Biblical Apocalypse?

N.H.: A deluge, perhaps.

B.B.: And who survives?

N.H.: I don't know. Maybe none of us.

Interview with Gino Sandri, General Secretary of the Priory of Sion.

B.B.: Is the Priory real?

G.S.: It's a real society. But the Priory of Sion has many layers. Since 1956, it decided to become a public organisation. There's been a message they've wanted to get out to a specific group: *You have certain things. We know you have these things. And we have certain things.*

B.B.: Documents?

G.S.: Yes, among other things.

B.B.: What are the secrets you're guarding?

G.S.: I can't answer that question. I just can't. This is a dangerous subject. There are two organisations, the Priory of Sion and the Catholic Church… Opus Dei. There is the good and the bad. Let me just say one thing. I can tell you that there are certain coded works of art, but you have to understand their significance.

B.B.: Can you briefly describe the structure of the Priory? How many members? How many circles? How many in the core? How many on the outside?

G.S.: There is a central circle. There is about ten people in it. Ten or twelve. There's other circles around it. There are other associations which are not members of the central circle, but were inspired by them. Right now, the list is closed, we are not accepting new members. There is a certain number of people who are to be in this circle, and once one leaves we will bring another person in. But right now, we are full.

B.B.: What's the total number of members?

G.S.: In the centre, about ten. And maybe forty around them.

B.B.: And are they located all around the world or just in France?

G.S.: It's not limited to France.

B.B.: Could you tell me the sort of people who are members today?

G.S.: You need to have a very strong moral character. A very strict spirit. A very pure soul. The selection is very rigorous. So, I've tried to answer all of your questions in such a way to not just give you the truth but to give you the means to work out the truth.

Interview with Pierre Plantard, former Grand Master of the Priory.

H.L.: Monsieur Plantard, is there still a secret at Rennes-le-Chateau?

P.P.: But the secret is not only at Rennes-le-Chateau, the secret is Rennes-le-Chateau.

H.L.: Will the treasure of Rennes-le-Chateau ever be found?

P.P.: Here you are speaking of a material treasure… We are not talking of a material treasure. Let us say, quite simply, that there is a secret in Rennes-le-Chateau and that it is possible that there is something else around Rennes-le-Chateau.

H.L.: And how does Poussin fit into this story?

P.P.: To be seen in the Poussin painting, there are certain revelations. Poussin was an initiate, and therefore created his painting as an initiate. But he is not the only one in this story. There are other characters. Through artistic expression the truth is concealed.

H.L.: Can you tell us whether the Priory of Sion still exists today?

P.P.: At this moment Sion still exists. One of its more recent members – One of its Grand Masters – was Jean Cocteau. Everyone knows this.

H.L.: Monsieur Plantard, over the centuries you have supported the Priory of Sion.

P.P.: We have supported Sion, and Sion has supported us.

H.L.: Us? Who is "Us"?

P.P.: I am speaking of the Merovingian line. For our line is descended from King Dagobert II. The Merovingians, it was they who made France. Without them there would be no France. The Merovingians will restore France.

Afterword:

I am indebted to Eric Mader-Lin for allowing me to publish the Priory correspondence. I would also like to thank Le Priéuré de Sion for making them available to the public. And thank you, reader, for purchasing my little book.

"Et in Arcadia Ego."

Printed in Great Britain
by Amazon

82766527R00058